T0389822

FROM CORN TO CEREAL

BY MARI SCHUH · ILLUSTRATED BY JEANINE MURCH

AMICUS ILLUSTRATED

is published by Amicus Learning, an imprint of Amicus
P.O. Box 227, Mankato, MN 56002
www.amicuspublishing.us

LIBRARY OF CONGRESS CATALOGING-IN-PUBLICATION DATA

Names: Schuh, Mari C., 1975- author. | Murch,
Jeanine Henderson, illustrator.

Title: From corn to cereal / by Mari Schuh ;
illustrated by Jeanine Murch.

Description: Mankato, MN : Amicus Illustrated, [2025] | Series: Who
made my lunch? | Includes bibliographical references. |
Audience: Ages 6-9 | Audience: Grades 2-3 | Summary: "A
child wonders where cereal comes from and learns about
the jobs of a corn farmer, a miller, and cereal factory workers
as they describe the steps in making cereal. A great story to
support farm-to-table education, this illustrated narrative
nonfiction book includes a world map of where corn is grown,
glossary, and further resources"— Provided by publisher.

Identifiers: LCCN 2024010612 (print) | LCCN 2024010613
(ebook) | ISBN 9798892001090 (library binding) | ISBN
9798892001670 (paperback) | ISBN 9798892002257 (ebook)

Subjects: LCSH: Corn—Processing--Juvenile literature. |
Cereals, Prepared—Juvenile literature.

Classification: LCC TP435.C67 S38 2025 (print) | LCC TP435.
C67 (ebook) | DDC 664/.756—dc23/eng/20240409

LC record available at https://lccn.loc.gov/2024010612

LC ebook record available at https://lccn.loc.gov/2024010613

EDITOR: Rebecca Glaser
SERIES DESIGNER: Kathleen Petelinsek
BOOK DESIGNER: Kim Pfeffer

Printed in China

FOR HARPER AND LILLY—M.S.

ABOUT THE AUTHOR

Mari Schuh's love of reading began with cereal
boxes at the kitchen table. Today she is the author
of hundreds of nonfiction books for beginning
readers. She lives in the Midwest with her husband
and their sassy house rabbit. Mari believes cereal
is great for breakfast, lunch, or dinner.

ABOUT THE ILLUSTRATOR

Jeanine Murch is an illustrator with a lifelong
love of art, books, and storytelling. She lives in
Pittsburgh, PA, with her husband, two children, and
the world's most snuggly pup, all of which inspire
her work. When she isn't making art, she's usually
daydreaming about her next travel adventure.

Cereal is a big part of breakfast. It's healthy and ready to eat. But what if you had to grow the grain yourself? And you had to make the cereal?

Grab a hat and get ready to farm in Illinois! Many breakfast cereals are made from corn. And Illinois is a top grower of corn in the United States.

In spring, plant the seeds. Drive a tractor to pull a machine called a planter. It plants the seeds in the right spots. Each seed has enough space to grow.

Workers also make cereal from grains like wheat, barley, oats, rice, and rye. But right now, we are growing corn for our cereal. Let's get started!

corn

oats

wheat

barley

rice

rye

The warm sun ripens the corn. Enjoy the bright colors now. In the fall, your corn stalks will be dry and golden brown. The corn kernels will be hard and dry. Then it's time to harvest.

To harvest, drive a machine called a combine. The combine cuts the corn plants row by row. It removes the husks and puts corn kernels into the hopper. It chops the corn plant and spreads it on the field.

After harvest, you might store the corn in a grain bin. Or you might take the corn to a grain elevator to sell it right away.

Next stop—the mill. You're now a mill worker, and you make sure machines do their jobs. Machines sift and clean the corn kernels. They remove the outer covering, the hull, from the kernels.

Machines separate the three parts of the corn kernels: the bran, germ, and endosperm. Now use the endosperm to make corn grits. Send the corn grits to a cereal factory. Away they go!

At the factory, you'll make sure machines mix the corn grits with water, salt, sugar, and malt. Then cook the corn grits with steam in a rotating pressure cooker. About two hours later, they are soft and golden.

Next, let the corn grits cool down. Then closely watch the corn grits travel on a conveyor belt. Some grits are stuck together. No problem! A machine breaks up the clumps.

Next, dry the corn grits. Machines do the hard work! Then let the grits cool down again.

Metal rollers flatten the grits. Presto! Now they are thin flakes. Other cereals will become different shapes. Some might become round puffs or squares.

Now the cornflakes are ready for toasting. A stream of hot air gently heats them. Give the cornflakes extra nutrients. Spray them with vitamins and minerals.

Inspect the cornflakes. Then pack the cooled cornflakes into bags and boxes. Send them to grocery stores for people to buy.

Almost done!

Thanks to the farmers, mill workers, and factory workers, you have crunchy cereal to eat. Open a box, and enjoy a bowl of cornflakes. More milk, please!

WHERE IS THE MOST CORN GROWN?

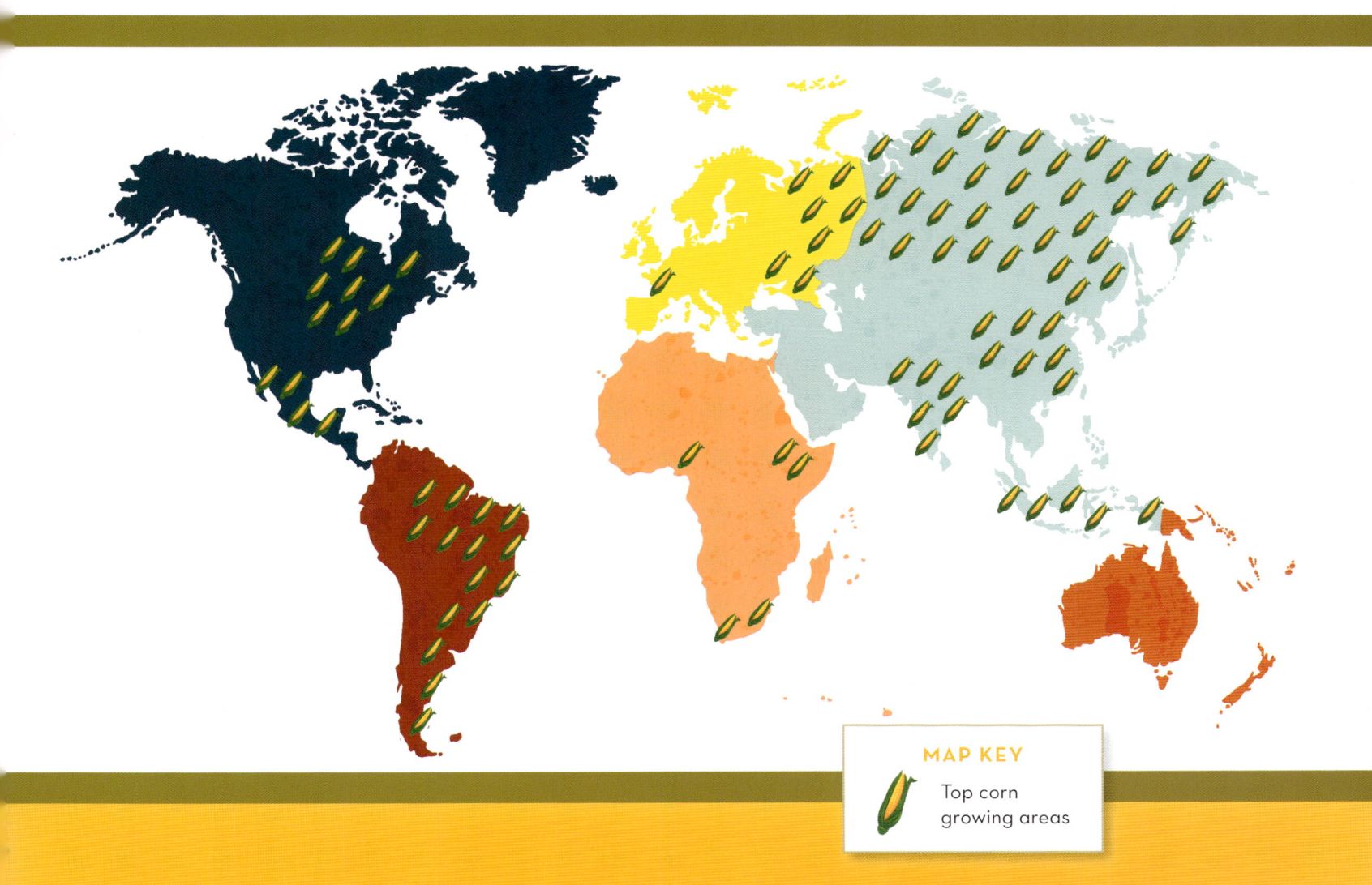

MAP KEY

Top corn growing areas

GLOSSARY

combine A machine that harvests corn by cutting it, separating the kernels, and putting the rest of the plant on the field.

grain elevator A very large building that stores grain.

hopper The part of a combine where grain such as corn is stored.

kernel A whole seed of corn.

nutrient Part of food that people need to eat to be healthy.

ripen Becoming fully grown and ready to eat.

toast To warm or heat thoroughly.

WEBSITES

Fueling My Healthy Life
https://www.fns.usda.gov/apps/TNinteractive/index.html
An activity from the USDA to learn about breakfast around the world.

Iowa Corn Fun for Kids
https://www.iowacorn.org/education/fun-for-kids
Enjoy fun activities from the Iowa Corn Growers Association.

Tiny Tap: Cereal
https://www.tinytap.com/activities/g1dcr/play/cereal
Games and activities to help you learn more about cereal.

Every effort has been made to ensure that these websites are appropriate for children. However, because of the nature of the Internet, it is impossible to guarantee that these sites will remain active indefinitely or that their contents will not be altered.

READ MORE

Koster, Gloria. *Grains Are Good for You!* North Mankato, Minn.: Pebble, 2023.

Nelson, Louise. *Healthy Eating.* Minneapolis: Jump!, Inc., 2024.

Reinke, Beth Bence. *Why We Eat Grains.* Minneapolis: Lerner Publications, 2019.